afraid hyperactive wild sad vulnerable uneasy bored scared curious prett

nasty lonely doubtful terrific exhausted excited rowdy zealous embarrasse

frightened giggly awful weird terrible quarrelsome crazy happ

zany disgusted intimidated greedy lucky friendly itchy jealous delighted hu

sweet vain jittery kind gross furious enthusiastic perturbed loving eager funn

zestful mischievous jumpy uncertain dizzy clever miserable

yucky nervous cool guilty nice anxious weak okay patient mad wacky excite

ashamed proud mixed-up pleased tired questionable ridiculous bashfu

energetic zonked rambunctious silly quiet overwhelme

negative sleepy glad insecure disappointed timid impatient joyful upse

sensitive vicious beautiful frustrated knowing irritable vibrant worried mood

generous exhilarated youthful active blue obnoxious calm afraid hyperactiv

wild sad vulnerable uneasy bored scared pretty nasty lonely doubtfu

terrific exhausted excited rowdy zealous embarrassed frightened brave

awful weird terrible quarrelsome crazy stubborn happy zany disguste

intimidated greedy lucky friendly itchy jealous delighted hurt sweet vai

jittery kind gross furious enthusiastic perturbed loving funny zestfu

mischievous jumpy keen uncertain dizzy clever miserable naughty yuck

nervous cool guilty nice anxious weak okay patient mad wacky excited ashame roud mixed-up pleased queasy tired questionable ridiculous bashful hopeful

nergetic different zonked rambunctious **silly** quiet overwhelmed

egative sleepy glad **insecure** disappointed selfish timid impatient joyful upset

ensitive vicious beautiful frustrated knowing irritable vibrant worried moody

enerous **exhilarated** active obnoxious **blue** calm afraid hyperactive

ild sad vulnerable uneasy bored scared curious pretty nasty **lonely** doubtful

rrific exhausted **excited** zealous embarrassed frightened brave giggly

wful weird terrible quarrelsome crazy stubborn **happy** zany disgusted

timidated greedy lucky friendly itchy **jealous** delighted hurt sweet vain

ttery **kind** furious enthusiastic perturbed loving eager funny zestful

ischievous jumpy keen uncertain **dizzy** clever miserable naughty yucky

ervous **cool** guilty nice anxious weak okay patient **wacky** excited ashamed

roud mixed-up pleased queasy tired questionable ridiculous **bashful** hopeful

nergetic different zonked **rambunctious** silly quiet overwhelmed

egative **sleepy** insecure disappointed selfish **impatient** joyful upset

ensitive vicious beautiful frustrated knowing irritable vibrant worried moody

enerous exhilarated youthful active blue obnoxious calm afraid hyperactive

ild **sad** vulnerable uneasy bored scared **curious** nasty lonely doubtful

rrific exhausted excited rowdy zealous embarrassed frightened brave **giggly** afraid hyperactive wild sad vulnerable uneasy bored scared curious pret

nasty lonely doubtful terrific exhausted excited rowdy zealous embarrasse

frightened giggly awful weird terrible quarrelsome crazy happ

zany disgusted intimidated greedy lucky friendly itchy jealous delighted hu

sweet vain jittery kind gross furious enthusiastic perturbed loving eager funn

zestful mischievous jumpy uncertain dizzy clever miserabl

yucky nervous cool guilty nice anxious weak okay patient mad wacky excite

ashamed proud mixed-up pleased tired questionable ridiculous bashf

energetic zonked rambunctious silly quiet overwhelme

negative sleepy glad insecure disappointed timid impatient joyful ups

sensitive vicious beautiful frustrated knowing irritable vibrant worried mood

generous exhilarated youthful active blue obnoxious calm afraid hyperactiv

wild sad vulnerable uneasy bored scared pretty nasty lonely doubtf

terrific exhausted excited rowdy zealous embarrassed frightened brav

awful weird terrible quarrelsome crazy stubborn happy zany disguste

intimidated greedy lucky friendly itchy jealous delighted hurt sweet va

jittery kind gross furious enthusiastic perturbed loving funny zestf

mischievous jumpy keen uncertain dizzy clever miserable naughty yuck

nervous cool guilty nice anxious weak okay patient mad wacky excited asham

LOTS OF Feelings

SHELLEY ROTNER

M Millbrook Press • Minneapolis

To my editor, Jean Reynolds,
who always makes me feel valued as an author and photographer.

Millbrook Press
A division of Lerner Publishing Group, Inc.
241 First Avenue North
Minneapolis, MN 55401 USA

For reading levels and more information, look up this title at www.lernerbooks.com.

LIBRARY OF CONGRESS CATALOGING-IN-PUBLICATION DATA
Rotner, Shelley.
Lots of feelings / Shelley Rotner.
p.   cm.
Summary: Simple text and photographs introduce basic emotions—happy,
grumpy, thoughtful, and more—and how people express them.
ISBN 978–0–7613–2896–4 (lib. bdg. : alk. paper)
ISBN 978–0–7613–2377–8 (pbk. : alk. paper)
ISBN 978–0–7613–2646–5 (EB pdf)
1. Emotions in children—Juvenile literature. [1. Emotions.] I.
Title.
BF723.E6R68 2003
152.4—dc21
2003006678

Manufactured in the United States of America
20 – CG – 10/1/15

We have lots of **feelings.**

Sometimes
we feel
happy,

4

sometimes sad.

5

Sometimes
we're
grumpy,

other
times
excited.

At times
we feel
shy

and
other
times
proud.

We
feel
angry
at
times

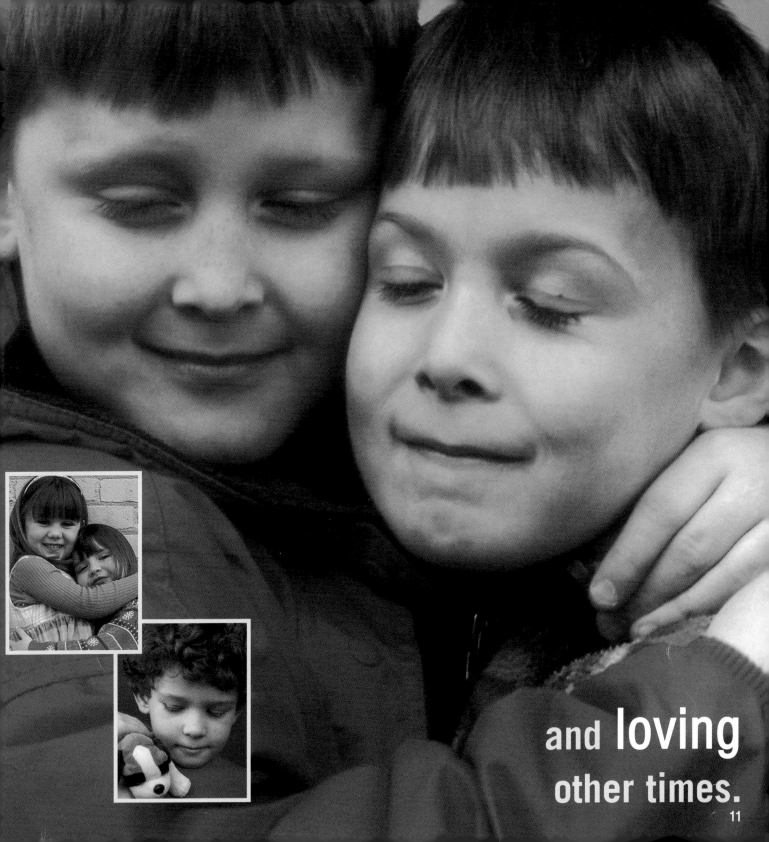

and **loving**
other times.

Some things surprise us.

Other things frighten us.

There are times
we feel
thoughtful

14

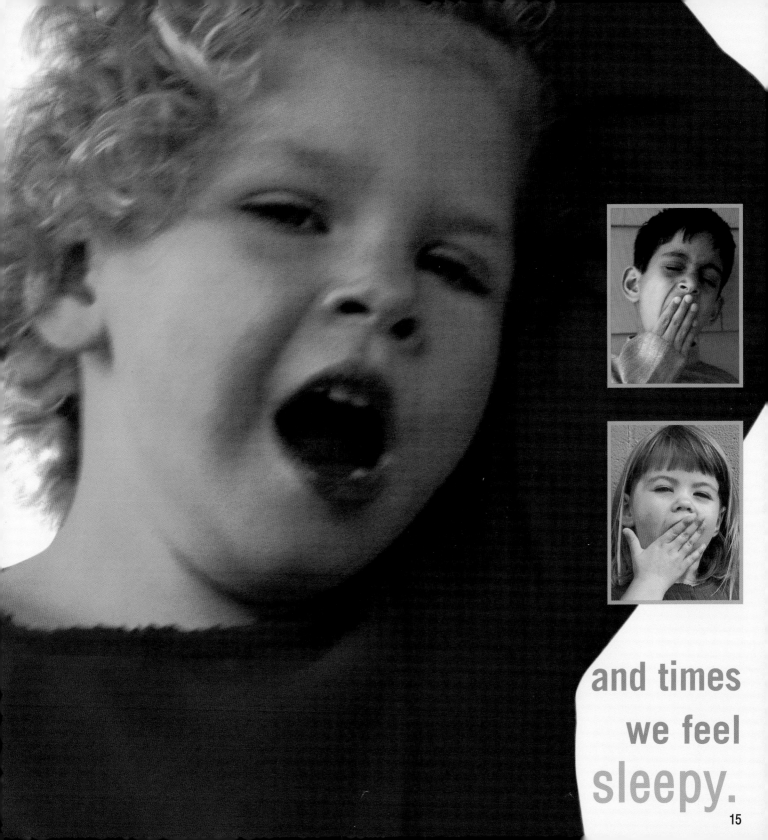

and times we feel sleepy.

At different times we feel

serious...

or silly...

curious...

or confused.

19

Everyone
has
lots of
feelings.

How about **you?**

NOTE FOR PARENTS OR TEACHERS

Lots of Feelings is a book to help children become more aware of their feelings. By learning how to express emotions in appropriate ways, they can better understand themselves and communicate what they are feeling to others. Parents and teachers can use this book to help generate conversation to facilitate this learning process.

Sometimes we don't know exactly how we feel or our faces don't reflect how we really feel inside. Yet how we express ourselves is how we are viewed by others. This is an opportunity for grown-ups to take the time to listen to how children feel and to guide them to appropriate expression so they can be heard and understood. The different faces throughout the book can be used as a means of identifying emotions.

Parents and teachers might use questions such as the following to explore feelings: "What do you think this boy/girl is feeling?" "Have you ever felt this way?" "What would make him feel that way?" "What do you think she would say?" Role playing is another way to help children practice forms of expression. Children can take turns acting out a feeling and their family or friends can respond.

The more we understand our own feelings the more we can understand others. Learning to understand the value of expressing his or her feelings appropriately is an important life skill for a young child and a key element in the development of good communication skills.

Shelley Rotner

fraid hyperactive wild sad vulnerable uneasy bored scared curious pretty

asty lonely doubtful terrific exhausted excited rowdy zealous embarrassed

ightened giggly awful weird terrible quarrelsome crazy happy

any disgusted intimidated greedy lucky friendly itchy jealous delighted hurt

weet vain jittery kind gross furious enthusiastic perturbed loving eager funny

estful mischievous jumpy uncertain dizzy clever miserable

ucky nervous cool guilty nice anxious weak okay patient mad wacky excited

shamed proud mixed-up pleased tired questionable ridiculous bashful

energetic zonked rambunctious silly quiet overwhelmed

egative sleepy glad insecure disappointed timid impatient joyful upset

ensitive vicious beautiful frustrated knowing irritable vibrant worried moody

enerous exhilarated youthful active blue obnoxious calm afraid hyperactive

ild sad vulnerable uneasy bored scared pretty nasty lonely doubtful

errific exhausted excited rowdy zealous embarrassed frightened brave

wful weird terrible quarrelsome crazy stubborn happy zany disgusted

ntimidated greedy lucky friendly itchy jealous delighted hurt sweet vain

ttery kind gross furious enthusiastic perturbed loving funny zestful

nischievous jumpy keen uncertain dizzy clever miserable naughty yucky

ervous cool guilty nice anxious weak okay patient mad wacky excited ashamed

25

afraid hyperactive wild sad vulnerable uneasy bored scared curious prett

nasty lonely doubtful terrific exhausted excited rowdy zealous embarrasse

frightened giggly awful weird terrible quarrelsome crazy happ

zany disgusted intimidated greedy lucky friendly itchy jealous delighted hur

sweet vain jittery kind gross furious enthusiastic perturbed loving eager funn

zestful mischievous jumpy uncertain dizzy clever miserable

yucky nervous cool guilty nice anxious weak okay patient mad wacky excite

ashamed proud mixed-up pleased tired questionable ridiculous bashfu

energetic zonked rambunctious silly quiet overwhelme

negative sleepy glad insecure disappointed timid impatient joyful upse

sensitive vicious beautiful frustrated knowing irritable vibrant worried mood

generous exhilarated youthful active blue obnoxious calm afraid hyperactiv

wild sad vulnerable uneasy bored scared pretty nasty lonely doubtfu

terrific exhausted excited rowdy zealous embarrassed frightened brave

awful weird terrible quarrelsome crazy stubborn happy zany disguste

intimidated greedy lucky friendly itchy jealous delighted hurt sweet v

jittery kind gross furious enthusiastic perturbed loving funny zes

mischievous jumpy keen uncertain dizzy clever miserable naughty yu

nervous cool guilty nice anxious weak okay patient mad wacky excited ashan

oud mixed-up pleased queasy tired questionable ridiculous bashful hopeful
nergetic different zonked rambunctious silly quiet overwhelmed
egative sleepy glad insecure disappointed selfish timid impatient joyful upset
nsitive vicious beautiful frustrated knowing irritable vibrant worried moody
enerous exhilarated active obnoxious blue calm afraid hyperactive
ild sad vulnerable uneasy bored scared curious pretty nasty lonely doubtful
rrific exhausted excited zealous embarrassed frightened brave giggly
wful weird terrible quarrelsome crazy stubborn happy zany disgusted
timidated greedy lucky friendly itchy jealous delighted hurt sweet vain
ttery kind furious enthusiastic perturbed loving eager funny zestful
ischievous jumpy keen uncertain dizzy clever miserable naughty yucky
ervous cool guilty nice anxious weak okay patient wacky excited ashamed
oud mixed-up pleased queasy tired questionable ridiculous bashful hopeful
nergetic different zonked rambunctious silly quiet overwhelmed
egative sleepy insecure disappointed selfish impatient joyful upset
nsitive vicious beautiful frustrated knowing irritable vibrant worried moody
enerous exhilarated youthful active blue obnoxious calm afraid hyperactive
ild sad vulnerable uneasy bored scared curious nasty lonely doubtful
rrific exhausted excited rowdy zealous embarrassed frightened brave giggly